The Bell Buckle Years

The Bell Buckle Years

NEW EDITION

Charlotte Barr

2011

Parson's Porch Books

Cleveland, Tennessee

Parson's Porch Books
121 Holly Trail Road, NW
Cleveland, Tennessee 37311

The Bell Buckle Years

Published 2011.
Printed in the United States of America.
ISBN 978-1-936912-05-6

To order additional copies of this book, contact:

Parson's Porch Books
1-423-475-7308
www.parsonsporchbooks.com

Photographic Credits:
Author photograph (back cover) — Brunner Studio, Berea, Kentucky
Cover Photograph — Charlotte Barr

Book design and cover art: Eric Killinger for *Ars Intermundia Expressus*

To the Eight from Webb:
Allen, Cindy, Jason, Jerry,
Laura Beth, Luke, Scott,
and Supriya,
who ventured with me into
the writer's world.
"Fare forward, voyagers!"

Table of Contents

Publisher's Note

Even more changes have occurred since Charlotte Barr published her first book of poetry, *Sister Woman*, with Britton James Publishers. The most recent of these is that Charlotte now publishes with Parson's Porch Books of Cleveland, Tennessee, the publishing venture that supports Parson's Porch, a not-for-profit 501(c)(3) charity organization that provides pastoral care and spiritual guidance to the poor and helps with monthly needs such as utility bills, rent, and other self-identified needs.

Another change is that she moved back to Chattanoga, Tennessee, where she was on the English faculty and poet in residence at The Baylor School. She retired from teaching in 2007 but continues to write poetry, her latest volume being *The Text Beneath*, published by Parson's Porch Books in 2010.

From 1990-1992, Charlotte lived in Bell Buckle, Tennessee, teaching English and Creative Writing at the prestigious Webb School. This collection of poems, *The Bell Buckle Years*, represents a major transition in the life and work of one of America's finest poets.

Spanning some three decades of convent life, the critically acclaimed *Sister Woman* celebrates both the vigilance and commitment to mystery present in our disorderly and often chaotic world. *The Bell Buckle Years* reflects transitions not only in the poet's environment but even more in her sense of self. Parson's Porch Books is proud to reissue this volume by such an important poet and looks forward to publishing future works.

Publisher's Note to the First Edition

In 1989, Charlotte Barr, then Sister Mary Anthony, published her first book of poetry, *Sister Woman*, with Britton James Publishers. Since that time, several changes have occurred. The owner of Britton James Publishers had the opportunity to purchase Iris Press, a small press of national importance, and Sister Mary Anthony is now publishing with Iris Press. The second change is that Sister Mary Anthony left the Dominican Order in 1990, and is now writing under her original name.

For the past two years, Charlotte has lived in Bell Buckle, Tennessee, and taught English and Creative Writing at the prestigious Webb School. This collection of poems, *The Bell Buckle Years*, represents a major transition in the life and work of one of America's finest poets.

The critically acclaimed *Sister Woman* spans thirty years of convent life and celebrates both the discipline and desire present in an orderly and confined world.

This new volume, *The Bell Buckle Years*, reflects not only a change in the poet's surroundings but even more in her sense of self. Iris Press continues to publish this important poet and looks forward to many works to come.

— Margaret Britton Vaughn
Iris Press

Preface

The poems in this collection are products of upheaval and dislocation which they, in some perhaps indefinable way, record. I came to the country from the convent, after

> Years of living among the breakage
> Of what was believed in as the most reliable—
> And therefore the fittest for renunciation.

These lines from Eliot's great prayer-poem, "Four Quartets," accompanied me, along with the baggage of three decades in a religious community. In the throes of a painful leave-taking, I settled into my uncertain niche within a boarding school community and my place in a tiny village traditionally receptive to artists and craftsmen. People have been kind and this transitional time has been good.

At first I thought that both Sister Mary Anthony and her Muse had stayed behind in Nashville. I began to fear that I might never be able to pray or to write poems again. But in time I came to understand that the Sister and the Woman were the same person, and that vows to God go deeper than any document. Our gifts are not revoked; in the soul's night they wait, among the unseen angels, to be summoned from the shadows and attend us. I learned to pray again, and since "waking in the country" I have begun to write again.

"So here I am," to borrow from Eliot once more,

> Trying to learn to use words, and every attempt
> Is a wholly new start, and a different kind of failure
> Because one has only learnt to get the better of words
> For the thing one no longer has to say, or the way in which
> One is no longer disposed to say it. And so each venture
> Is a new beginning, a raid on the inarticulate . . .
> Here and there does not matter
> We must be still and still moving
> Into another intensity.

Meanwhile, I owe some debts of gratitude and want to pay them here. Thanks to my family, Margaret, David, and Nelson Barr, for supporting my decision and welcoming me home. Thanks to the people of Bell Buckle for their gracious reception of an urban refugee. Many thanks to Jon Frere and the The Webb School for allowing me to have two years among them. Thanks for Brunner Studio of Berea, Kentucky, for the back cover photograph. And of course, my gratitude to Maggi Vaughn, publisher of this volume's first edition and friend, for convincing me I could do this book and chaining me to the desk.

— Charlotte Barr
Bell Buckle, Tennessee
February 1992

Editor's Foreword to the New Edition

And the Master said to his guest:
"May you find your place."
"Where is my place?"
"In the center of your soul."
"How can I get there?
"It seems an entire lifetime would not be enough to reach it."
And the Master said:
"You have reached it. I can tell by your divine pallor."
"I stand before you, split in two.
"On one side, me; on the other side, me. In the middle, nothing."
And the Master said:
"That is your place."

— Edmond Jabès, *A Foreigner Carrying in the Crook of His Arm a Tiny Book*

I first encountered the poetry of Charlotte Barr in September 2010, when I was assigned as her editor during my own transition to the role of publisher for Parson's Porch Books. The manuscript, as it was submitted to me, was tentatively and simply entitled, *Poems: 1992–2010*. Fine. But I was informed we wanted the book to be marketable.

I recall our flurry of e-mails. Always gracious when dealing with my editorial inquiries and overall book design, Charlotte impressed me even more with her love, and more importantly, her dance with language. In the end, Charlotte invited me to cobble together a suitable title. There were three words that popped into my mind then and even now they capture for me the essence of Charlotte's poems: *the text beneath*. These three words subsequently became the title for her book that I was editing at the time.

Near the end of 2010, I was approached with the idea of bringing out a new edition of *The Bell Buckle Years*. As indicated in the Publisher's note, Parson's Porch Books is proud to publish this new edition of Charlotte's second volume of poetry (Parson's Porch Books is also releasing a new edition of her first volume, *Sister Woman*, this spring).

This volume, *The Bell Buckle Years*, is particularly significant for the way it deals with transitions, those places between me on the one side and me on the other. It's the bit between that's important. Wasn't it mythologist Joseph Campbell who constantly pointed out that it wasn't the destination—on the other side, me—that was so important, but rather the journey? This, it seems to me, is why Charlotte Barr's facility with language belies an immense depth.

"Biblical growth means going down," as begins the poem, "At Fifty." Such depth is not frightening in the sense of Nietzsche's dictum of how, when staring long into the abyss, we find it staring—perhaps even *glaring*—back at us. No. We are brought into a mode of receptivity that allows the work(s) of the poet to envision us by palpating and encircling our hearts rather than our having questions to hand for which we seek answers. It is a loving, enveloping depth that holds, bathes, and releases rather than drowns us. This is in keeping with the maintenance of this between, this space for possibilities, since—as the late French essayist and literary critic Maurice Blanchot was wont to remind us—*La résponse est le malheur de la question*. The answer is the dis-ease of curiosity, its adversity.

To be sure, the enveloping that we experience in this collection of poems mediates stillness, something so necessary in these fast-paced, increasingly difficult lives and times in which we seem to thrive, move, and have our being. Yet we are also afforded an experience of *anamnesis*, the work of un-forgetting, as what was or has been forgotten is re-awakened, given, and heard with soul in mind. I think here of the poem, "Recollection," which begins by recalling Proust's having brought the practice of recall to high art in his multi-volumed continuous novel, *A la recherche du temps perdu* (properly interpolated as *Re-search of Lost Time*), and "ends" with a continuous heartbeat.

Anamnesis—recollection—is important for us as transitions are difficult processes in and of themselves, for they begin with endings. Charlotte Barr invoked Eliot in the preface, and he might be called forth here as well:

> What we call the beginning is often the end
> And to make an end is to make a beginning.
> The end is where we start from.
>
> — T. S. Eliot, "Little Gidding"

Endings signal that a death, a *thanatos*, of sorts is involved. Charlotte Barr speaks of this in her preface in terms of the upheaval brought about by leaving her order and moving to new surroundings, wondering if she could write, let alone pray and live.

Transitions, then, are virtually synonymous with *crisis*. Yes, but isn't the Chinese pictograph for crisis made up of two parts? The one is "danger," and it depicts a person on the edge of a precipice. The other is "opportunity," represented by a tree standing next to a table or perhaps a loom. Crisis reminds us that even in danger a prospect, however seemingly insignificant, is still a passage, a way to work *through* the danger. Again, what is important is that bit between. On the one side, me. On the other side, me. In the middle, nothing?

Ah, this between, though not a thing, is an entity. Specifically, it is an event of folding and unfolding. There is, as we know full well in life, pliability, even flexibility.As with the painter in "The Canvas Out of Doors,"

> The canvas will be kept indoors.
> You will ever seek the light and find
> In the pursuit surfeit of life.

Yet this flexibility, this pliability we ourselves cannot possess. It possesses us. In these poems, we are opened to a dimension that can never again be closed because of our being between. Ontological twaddle? Not really, since the liminality of this no-thingness that is our place is pre-ontological at best—even nonascertainable.

George Core, in his foreword to the first edition of *Sister Woman*, commented as how enthusiastic he was to learn of Charlotte Barr's poetry fifteen years before the book's publication and just as enthusiastically commended and passed *Sister Woman* on to future generations of readers. I wholeheartedly recommend *The Bell Buckle Years* to you. Carry it with you in the crook of your arm. Take time to sit with the poems within its pages. Let them wash over you, linger with and fill you with their recreating power. You might just discover your place and re-search the journey to the center of your soul.

— Eric Killinger
Editor and Publisher,
Parson's Porch Books
April 2011

Waking in the Country

One would think the rooster's cry contrived:
It is so cued to dawn, so classical,
A cold red sound of morning
To which I stumble out with coffee
To my porch, where the mist lifts
Out of the drained pond's basin
Into day.

Hay bales wait like bread loaves
Buttered with dew for the August sun
To brown them:
Toast for the cows I always hear
But do not see, in some neighbor's
Holding pen.

I smell them too, their rich dark offal
Steaming off the grass,
Imagining their faces
Lolling under trees with eyes
Like pools of acquiescence,
Their teats so many patient fingers
Waiting to be squeezed alive.

My life has lingered thus:
For tugs upon the dreaming heart,
For sundered ties, for peace.
Far from here I thought I lived.
This morning, waking here,
I'm pulled from dreams I died in
Into life.

The Death of Cousins

I am perhaps thinking too precisely
On the event, Death having visited my
Tribe twice this year: the maternal
Side, the father's, tit for tat.
This, at last, is my generation, this
I feel is more than grief; it's our
Mortality, mine, my brothers', the
Cousins left to us, which is not many
(We modern families tending as we do
To put all our eggs in one basket).

The mirror magnetizes me, shows what's
Left of me, but does not explicate the
Images: gray hair gathering at the part,
Grooved cheek, despair of opening other
Doors, and yes, it's trite but true,
The existential angst, stare back at me.

Mirror, mirror, tell me whether entropy
Is all.

Late winter brings an early Lent this year.
I used to think I could fast and satisfy
Thereby the deeper hunger, pray and strive
And by such striving redesign myself, my
Metanoia.

It is mild for February, though I suspect
That Winter has a few more cards to play
Before the green blade rises.

Memories rise before me: the cousins with us
At our games of tag, distant voices chanting,
"All fall down!"
This is what I know of death, then:
Time is called, our mothers call us hoome,
All fall down and one does not get up.

Congenial Heart Defects

The pet store man repeated the phrase,
Assuring me that such contingencies
Are covered by the warranty.
The teacher in me yielded to the poet,
Letting the malappropriate line go
Uncorrected, relishing it as grist
For the mill, singing it to myself
On the way home: O happy faults,
Harmonious happenstance, congenial
Defects of birth, the cardial flaw!

Since coming to live with me, my puppy
Shows no sign of illness, congenital
Or acquired; his heart is steady and
Beloved of mine, which leaves me with
A healthy dog and this coinage of the
Salesman hankering for a context,
A bed of words to lie in now outside
My brain; how's this: a meditation
On the sicknesses that flesh is heir to?
But that's been done. Then this: the
Ills we love and dote on more than dread?

Listening to my dog's heart and my own,
Late at night, no human presence near,
I lie abed and list for fun the friendly
Foes that I have overthrown; or forces
Both forgotten and forgiven which I have
Knelt to, decrees by which my soul was
Driven and were, had I but known, mere

Words with mortal meanings like my own.
My pet store man said more than he was
Able: how seldom augury's defied, yet
Sometimes the page will bear a slight
Syllable shift, a variant spelling, a
Word reordered here and there.

Polished Floors

Unbidden,
The convent loomed up
From my just waxed floor.
And thirty years of life
Were in the scent of
Mineral spirits and
Polished hardwood floors.
Three years gone, those
Times of cleaning before
A major feast, those
Festal days spread with
Chant and merriment,
But here again, just now,
And from now on,
As ingrained as
The pattern in
The bole.

Of Virgins

Purity abides not long
In those who gauge it,
Measuring virtue's weight
Against their own, but casts
Her eye upon the hindmost
Parts of Christendom, the
Prodigals; she too subsists
On famine's husks, the bare
Habiliment of hope.

The worst is not to sleep
Alone, but is to make of
Solitude a haven for the
Unencumbered self; the
Virgin who's not merely
Chaste, but clean of heart,
Knows this: her hunger is
Antecedent to the feast,
Her vacancy invites the
Playfulness of God.

Teaching Hamlet Again

Each year it is the same story:
Attempting to report the Prince's cause
Aright, I sail to Elsinore with my reluctant
Crew, who, put off by ghosts, kings, and
Ministers of grace, resist the page, the
Plodding work, Elizabethen turns of phrase,
Preferring their familiar food to this rich
Feast of words, words, words.
Still the magic has its will of them:
Step-parents, sexual tensions, soul-deep
Fears take hold while, List, list, oh list,
I plead, and spill the potent passages,
Dire distillment of the poet's wizardry,
Into their ears.

The dream of eale,
The vicious mole of nature need no
Footnote, nor need I say that Hamlet is
Ourselves; any one of them, for all their
Adolescent artlessness, can understand
That we are worse than mothers think us,
Yet, being adamites, matter more to God
Than all the uncorrupted nebula
Of sinless space.

Unnerved and altered,
Beset by beauty's other face,
My class holds dying Hamlet to its breast
And is unsatisfied by fifth-act resolutions.

The play's the thing they hadn't thought
Could shift the planets, rock their
Spaceship, Earth, and bring them home
So changed from what they knew.

At voyage's end,
Grades are given and received and we go on,
Fortinbras securely on the throne, cries of
Havoc stilled, the syllabus for Shakespeare
Stowed until another gang of Janes and Joes
Embarks with me beyond the bounds of their
Philosophy.

Rumination

Man is a cow parasite.
— Kundera

To ruminate is both to think and chew,
So here among the ruminants I muse
On things that cattle and humans do.
We think, they chew; but why excuse
Our mastication, our potency to fuse
Thought with appetite and make of two
Abilities one animal, who can abuse
All others, sheltering in their skin
The refugee from Eden and his sin?

Choices

What was not chosen is not lost,
All that I renounced becomes my gain,
I get it free who thought to pay the cost.

This clasp, that spurn, here keep, there toss,
The world spins on despite my joy or pain,
What was not chosen is not lost.

Apart from my deciding comes the frost,
No word of mine sends down the warming rain,
I get it free who thought to pay the cost.

Some was gold I saved and some was dross,
The blessing fell in tandem with the bane,
What was not chosen is not lost.

Friends turn foe while foes the heart accost,
Love resides where lover has never lain,
I get it free who thought to pay the cost.

The roads I never took I later crossed,
Who thought directions guided by the brain.
What was not chosen is not lost,
I get it free who thought to pay the cost.

The Canvas Out of Doors

for Todd

Hugging on the lawn after your commencement,
Your painting loomed between us, its bold
Swirls of red and purple, stroked hard and
Deep indoors, a winter's work, and now a
Fence of light.

It did not hold apart but joined at the
Heart teacher and student, friend and friend,
Lattice-like, our arms above it twined like
Summer's vines.

Laden as it was with heavy oils and youth's
Dark secret nights, you canvas was porous:
For all the love seeped through, the consequential
Things that are not said in school, the hopes
Saved for May's last morning, the prayers your
Elders want to spread down all the roads you go.

This piece, held lightly in your slender hands
Against the green-gold lawn, in its frameless
Innocence framed us, the poet and the painter.

You, with your appraising eye, saw the sunshot
Colors shimmering and said, "It looks better
Out of doors. It needs a lot of light."

Where were you taking it, I wondered, and was told
You meant to hang it in your girlfriend's room.
I hoped she'd have a window facing it, so did you.

I didn't say I doubted your hometown girl could
See what your eyes see, or ever know how much
Your soul needs light.

For you, dear painter, I don't foresee sufficient
Light, but Life, oh yes!

The palette is prepared with agony and bliss,
Not happiness nor ease nor recognition;
The canvas will be kept indoors.
You will ever seek the light and find
In the pursuit surfeit of life.

Grace

I am dying, as I have lived, beyond my means.
— Oscar Wilde

Knowing his guest would never pay,
The Paris hotelier sent champagne.
Sure he would not survive the day,
The priest had only a soul to gain
And proffered the holy viaticum,
Per omnia saecula saeculorum.
The poet fell silent at eventide,
Hands and lips now cold and dumb.
Let all applaud, let all deride,
His ears were deaf to man's acclaim.
Neither knew he more of shame,
But, unencumbered, fled those walls
And wandered free of praise or blame,
Beyond the gossip, glare, and brawls,
Out of his depth, in Mercy's place,
Utterly beyond his means, in Grace.

The Veterans

I have seen wars, I have seen wars,
give thy heart after letters.
— Egyptian sage

From the Veterans Home the old men walk to town,
Through Railroad Square, to the P. O. and café;
Behind them Susie comes, the bluetick hound,
Arthritic as her masters, and as true as they.

What wars and warrior's griefs have these men seen,
What ragged scars do their thin jackets hide?
What would they tell us honor and valor mean,
Would they prefer to be the ones who died?

Gray is the ash line on their cigarettes,
Gray is the stubble on their narrow chins;
The nation pays their pension and forgets
How Time divests its heroes of their wins.

THE HERB GARDEN

The Herb Garden

Planting these herbs beside my secular fence,
Behind my profane dwelling, under the vulgar sky,
I remember cloistered monastery gardens
And smile to the sun that shines on sinners
As on saints:
I plant them all for remembrance.

I. Basil

My little kings,
Two Basils grow together,
The dark opal and the sweet.
Basil, your oval leaves,
One green, the other purple,
WIll mimic mint and clove,
Your blossoms show the eye
False whorls when you are
Grown: *Ocimum basilicum*
From India and *Mare Nostrum,*
I will be deceived
Gladly, gladly.

11. Catnip

My catmint is heart-shaped
And downy, of gray-green
Leaf and purple flower spikes.
My cat does not love you,
Indifferent to you allure,
Nepeta cataria.
But I will dote on you,
Crush you to garner your store,
The feline in me tantalized,
Teased, willing to be
Catnip-pleased.

III. Chervil

Here is curled chervil,
Whose feather leaves
On slender stems will taste
Of anise and tarragon.
Anthriscus cerefolium,
You were carried by the Legions
Through the Alps and prized
By cooks in France.
I prize you, though you want to
Go to seed in midsummer.
Stay, my chervil, stay.

IV. Dill

The classic crown of heroes
Was my *Anethum graveolens,*
Borne from the East,
With her lacy blue-green leaves,
Her yellow flowers.
My umbrella-head, my garland,
There is more to you
Than marriage with a pickle,
Dilly, dilly, my dear.

v. Fennel

Behold the bronze fennel,
Hard-seed spice of the
Egyptians.
My tender perennial,
I love your name:
Foeniculum vulgare dulce.
You are sweet, not vulgar,
Lacey licoricey fennel,
Foeniculae, foeniculorum.

vi. Hyssop

O my ancient one!
Cleanse me with hyssop and
I shall be cleansed,
Wash me and I shall be
Whiter than snow.
Hyssopus of the purification!
Bees and butterflies love thee
No less than monks and patriarchs.
My hardy one, whose
Mint-mocking leaves
Will shoot out spikes
Of blue and pink and white.
Who else but you has panicles
And squarrose stems and
Branching rootstock?

VII. Marjoram

Sweet *Origanum majorana,*
I touch your delicate hairs,
Your lavender-pink florets,
Bursting from knots along
Your slender stem.
Fruitful marjoram,
Queen of Sicily,
Crown of the nuptial bed!
Be happy in my garden.
Let one share of your double
Bliss fall on this single head.

VIII. Parsley

I have you both,
The curly and the flat,
Crispum crispum and
Crispum neapolitanum.
Your abundance makes you
Common, little *Petroselinum,*
Decorative and disregarded.
But the ancients found you
Festive when you smiled
Upon their banquets and
Sweetened their winey air.
You survived the banqueters
To be the garnish on our lives.

IX. Pennyroyal

Look at my pennyroyal mint,
Admittedly a lesser one
Among the four hundred,
But more than a cent's worth
To me, my royal penny.
Do not deride her; though
She will not spice my tea,
She will deter a flea.
Mentha pulegium, hail to thee!

x. Rosemary

Here's rosemary for remembrance.
Rosmarinus, my piney dear,
Your scent is of Christmasses
Far and near, of forgotten
Faces mirrored in your boughs.
In my mind's eye your pale
Blue blossoms are dancing
By the Southern Sea.
Prick my memory, rosemarie,
Lest all I've known be
Drowned with poor Ophelia
And lost in Lethe's reedy bed.

XI. Sage

Are you wise, *Salvia officinalis*?
And why, it is said, should a man die
When sage flourishes in his garden?
These gray-green grainy leaves,
Shall they be tea, or stuffing
For the baking bird?
Cherished along the cloister paths,
Tended along the window sill,
Do you envy your brushy cousin
Of the western hills, and dream
Of blowing in the desert wind?

XII. Thyme

Aromatic *Thymis*, pungent one,
The hungry bees adore you.
Monks loved you too and bore
You over Alps to plant your
Woody taproot by their walls.
Singers say you spread your
Charm upon Scarborough Fair
In medieval times, with your
Companions, Parsley, Sage and
Rosemary too.
I say you and they and all
Your savory clan do more than
Sweeten meats, you sweeten
Minds.

My herbs, you green and gentle me;
I abjure my garish heart before your subtlety.

The Herb Gardener Warns Against Waging Mullein Wars

A friend said she spent her rural childhood
Waging war on mullein; that was her chore,
Stalking the proud yellow heads, dismayed
That they seeded the more the more she slew.
To my frontier friend mullein was a noxious
Plant, a tare, a weed, stealing her greenest
Joys, the shadow across the shining meadows
Of boysenberry days.

In England one June I saw mullein blooming
In the wolds and guarding the manor home,
Glinting along the drive in helms of gold.
Herbal lore tells me that mullein thrives
In any soil it can; that it can rinse
Sunlight into hair; that it consorts with
Lady's Mantle, the fairies, alas not we,
Can see them dance.

My friend of the mullein wars had bright
Hair once that now is drab and gray.
She became a teacher and children read
For her or else they cry; many's the
Tender plant that's blighted in those
Mullein-hardened hands; her classroom
Is a garden where no weeds ever grow:
You will be a rose or you will die.

Il faut que l'herbe pousse et que les enfants meurent.

Eros at Easter

He ran like a giant exulting on his way and came to the marriage bed of the cross, . . . and he joined himself to the woman forever.

— St. Augustine

What I've tried to say is this:
Eros drives the search for God,
Or else the heart is unredeemed.
It is his salt upon our tongue
That makes us thirst for him,
But there is more: He thirsts
For us.

This is what I see: Christ
Ransacking Hell to find his
Bride; he limps through Limbo's
Corridors; his soul is pale,
Wrenched clean from ligament
And lung and brain; he does not
Rest until each filament of
Flesh is washed and worn again:
"Behold and see that I am not
A ghost."

Though some would more adore
A god divided from the bone
Than he, who joys in matter,
Flowers through the stone,
Is wedded to the progeny of
Eve, I say not all of Passion
Is the pain.

Agape strained to this intensity
Is Eros and finds its uttermost
Declension in the cross; divinity
Exults in us or we are lost, and
Our religion only leaves the
Stone that seals the grave
Implacably in place.

Recollection

As Proust's madeleine and herbal tea
Were poised like faithful souls
Awaiting their moment, so for us all
The taste and smell of things unlocks
What was cedar-chested, folded and
Hidden from ourselves; our animal
Senses, ethereally persistent, evoke
Remembrnces against our will: old
Rancors, heart's ache or ease, places
Such as schools where all the early
Lessons were unlearned, but not the
Olio of chalk, crayola, pencil dust,
Gym clothes laden with pubescent
Exertion and desire.
From such a school I came as bearer
Once; I took a polo shirt a boy had
Left behind and gave it to his mother.
The child now dead, I thought to
Solace her by adding one late item
To the catalogue of flotsam washed
Ashore (I use the metaphor because
He died at sea); but she held the
Fabric in both hands, then raised
It to her face, inhaled, exhaled, and
Said, "It's been too long, it doesn't
Have his smell." It was a sorrow
Added to the other: Time had neutralized
The scent of boy, his dozen years of
Being quick and lithe, the perfume of
His sunny days and ways, as though the

Sea's obliteration had needed increment.
But the mnemonics of the nose persists;
And love persists, deeper than the
Valleys of the sea, the old diastolic
And systolic heart.

The Mind Revisits the Mother of the World

In the *Thousand and One Nights* she is
Misr um al-dunya, Mother of the World.
And many nights in memory have I gone
To her, the city where we dwelt a year
As though in tents, to *al–Qahira,*
The Triumphant.

Was it because she was a caravansary,
Receiving nomads all these centuries,
That Cairo held us in her dusty lap,
Let us lean against her ample breasts,
And then so lightly let us go?

At times in sleep a voice says, Rise
And go with me and let us linger on
The Nile Corniche, beside the nonpareil
Of rivers, flowing as no other flows.
I stand in reverie and pay my homage;
But I do not think to know how worshiped
Of the fellahin she is, how they in their
Feluccas dote on her.

On the Nile's east bank lies Maadi, where
I went to school, but it was all a school:
Land, alluvium, Arabian plateau, the
Cities of the dead, the living friends
I had and had to leave.

The heart in retrospect embraces all:
Backsheesh beggars and Gezira's rich,
French friars and Aswan's Russian engineers.

No less than Karnak's wonders were the
Muski's, where vendors sipped their Turkish
Coffee and reedy voices wailed on static-
Ridden radios; did Pharaoh's blood still
Flow in the black-veiled women haggling
Over fly-blown flanks of mutton? If
Alexander's dust could stop a hole, then
Why not trace a royal line to them?

I think of them in Ramadan, how they
Hungered until the cannon on the Citadel
Said, Eat; all the long spring they fasted;
And as the days wore on leaned irascibly
Upon their horns, cursing car and ass and
Camel in congested streets, or clung to
Buses stacked with scrawny chickens and
Allah's starved Cairenes.

The Moqattam Hills are still a landscape
For my dreams; and so too are the desert
Rides at dawn, when we rode the lip of
Morning south from Giza to Saqqara; the
Arabians, rented for a day, skittish and
Snorting sand, could stretch their withers
And bring us in three hours to the Pyramid
Of Sokkar; they were not mere horses, they
Were steeds, nay centaurs, and could fly
Up that stone staircase to the sky; and
We astride them thought all prizes were
As nigh, a few kilometers; tommorow then
Seemed but a short day's ride.

Two Sonnets

I. BLACK AND WHITE

No dress or attitude admitted gray,
It was albescent day, nigrescent night,
It was a perfect world of black and white;
To one stupendous choice we said our yea,
And after that we gave our wills away,
In *contemptus mundi,* straining toward the light,
We labored bell to bell, and put to flight
All terrors of the night and foes of day.
Dead to the world, the world was dead to us,
The rainbow's promise came without the sign;
To earthly joy as much as earthly lust
Our guarded eyes and shoruded hearts were blind;
Creation's loveliness did see but dust, .
The pale bread godlier than the purple wine.

II. COLOR

Christ's red redemption of a world in sin
Transformed the spectrum to a wheel of grace;
He took the maculate in his embrace,
And called our mottled mortal hearts his kin.
And so to color I have come again,
The sphere of black and white is not my place;
O let my piebald brush and palette trace
The hue of flower, fur and mackerel fin.
The poet's vesture is a motley coat,
And so in iridescence dwells the saint;
If vision prophet saw or poet wrote
Should bear no vestiges of human taint,
Then God should hot have formed the ark to float
Nor left his son upon the cross to faint.

At Fifty

I stand before my background like a tree.
— Rilke

Biblical growth means going down,
Sinking roots, weathering the storm;
In paticle physics everything is found
To have a use once it has a form.
Much seed falls on fertile ground,
I find that fig can even come from thorn;
Some fruit is bad and yet the tree is sound,
My leaf is green although the roots are torn.

Growing to Green

Once, autumn was the season of my blood,
When woodsmoke snaked along my arteries
And clogged my heart with primal ecstasy,
Before my dreams were laid on pyres of
Ochre and vermillion leaf, and curled,
And cried their scalded tears, and fled.

My goblet brimmed with crush of damask
Grape; I loved alone the erubescent rose
And spurned the limeloveliness of May.
My universe was bright and bold and red,
I scorned the pastel signature of spring.

Now that my own November hastens on, and
Winter's mantle soon will garment me,
The mind, which loves best what is gone,
Finds it behovely to be glad of green
For freen betokeneth hope; the final
Joy is the simple fact of grass.

Charlotte Barr was born in Knoxville, Tennessee, and spent her childhood in Chattanooga. She was a Dominican Sister in the Saint Cecilia Congregation in Nashville, Tennessee, from 1960 until 1990. For two years she lived in Bell Buckle and taught at the Webb School. Her first book of poems, *Sister–Woman*, was published in 1989 and reissued by Parson's Porch Books in 2011. Charlotte most recently taught at The Baylor School in Chattanooga, Tennessee, where she was on the English faculty and poet in residence. Her latest collection of poems, *The Text Beneath*, published in 2010, is also available from Parson's Porch Books.

www.ingramcontent.com/pod-product-compliance
Lightning Source LLC
LaVergne TN
LVHW050945080826
845145LV00004B/1412
* 9 7 8 1 9 3 6 9 1 2 0 5 6 *